♪♫Songs in the Night

- Tracy L. Moore

♪♫Songs in the Night by Tracy L. Moore

All scriptures are from the King James Version.

All inquiries should be addressed to:
Tracy L. Moore
PO Box 970284
Miami, FL. 33197-0284
786.473.3804
tra3moo@aol.com

Poem Contributions: Gerard McBean of New York

ISBN: 0-9646927-0-8

Library of Congress Cataloging-in-Publication Data
Moore, Tracy L.
Songs in the Night / Tracy L. Moore, TX 4-137-003

Printed in the United States of America

Original book cover by Randolph R. Waterman of Brooklyn, New York

Photo taken at: Simmons Collection African Arts Museum, 1063 Fulton Street, Brooklyn, NY 11238. Stanfield Simmons, Owner, Director & Curator.

He that knows not and knows that he knows not is a child: teach him.

He that knows not and knows not that he knows not is a fool: avoid him.

He that knows and knows not that he knows is asleep: awaken him.

He that knows and knows that he knows is wise: learn from him.

African Proverb

TABLE OF CONTENTS

The Essence (or Dignity) of a Man

There's something vital about each man!

Regardless of how high the heights…
(but especially) how low the levels…
Or how deep the depths…
That he finds himself,
When a dire emergency arises and it becomes
Inevitable
That his life be touched by another individual's:

I've found out that the ones
Authorized to perform emergency duties,
Do so with expertise.

Although they may be repulsed by the very
Sight of him,
Sound of him,
Smell of him…

They reach out, however grudgingly, and help.

In that instance, that man is important.

The essence of who he is – a human being – validates him and
Though it may be for a moment or maybe just for an hour,
In that instance, HIS LIFE COUNTS!

Ironically, this should be the case any day….
Under any circumstance.

For….he, too, is a man!

Palm Sunday, 4/4/93

Sunday, 12/29/2013: I wrote this while working at the Port Authority Bus Terminal (PABT) in the heart of Midtown Manhattan (New York). I began my shift at 6 or 7 am that morning on the subway level of the South Wing. Immediately after I entered the information booth, several patrons approached to complain about the horrible smell in the building. They pointed to a homeless man who was lying down on the floor not far from the booth. The patrons felt he should not be in the building, especially since the stench that emanated from him made it horrible to breathe. He was dressed in rags and looked like he had not had a bath for days. I went over to the man and asked if he was okay. He did not answer and I realized that he was ill. I called the PABT Police from my telephone. Within minutes several officers arrived and they then called for Emergency Medical Service (EMS). While we waited for EMS to arrive, several negative comments and jokes were directed at the homeless man. However, once EMS arrived, the saving of a life took on new meaning. They donned gloves and attended to the man. They checked his vitals, hooked him up to IV and took him away on a stretcher bound for a nearby hospital. This moved me to tears. The compassion shown shone brighter than the darkness and the hope verbally expressed swiftly muted and drowned out the complaints of patrons whose chief concerns were to get to their destinations as quickly as possible without the inconvenience of the blight and plight of the homeless.

On a philosophical note…

Regardless of what station or status in life that each of us finds himself or herself, the

ESSENCE of who we are – human beings – validates and makes each of us count. Each

of us is worthy and deserves to be heard and treated with respect.

Saturday, 10/9/93

For the Love of…

For the love of God
        I'll help my fellowman.

For the love of you
        I'll do whatever I can.

For the love of me
        I'll be the best that I am.

Saturday, 2/20/93

The ABCs of a Particular Man

Ambitious. **A**
Black man; a **B**ulwark and pillar of strength,
Challenging others to not give in to
Despair but to **D**ream **D**reams and to achieve them. A man of **D**istinction.
Effervescent:
Full of "joie de vivre" yet he can be as
Gentle as a lamb.
Hardworking and
Industrious: he is a man of strong character and good moral
Judgment; the essence of dignity!
Kindhearted....
Loyal....a
Militant in his own right.
Noble and
Outstanding, he is a
Proud descendant of
Queens and Kings – a
Reflection of the Creator and a **R**eminder to the world that in
Spite of the **S**tigma of **S**lavery and the **S**truggles

(because) of **S**egregation,
These are not what validate him…**T**hat he is, in fact,
Unique – a man of
Valor.
With these traits, this "Particular Black Man" is truly
'**X**traordinary!
You have reached **Y**our
Zenith- keep looking up.

Tuesday, 12/14/93

(Friday, January 03, 2014:
For R.E.D., you know who you are. Thanks for always believing in me, pushing me to pursue my dreams, even when I "outgrew" you – your words. You really saw me; you really "got" me and needed no explanation.)

Hear the Children

Can't you hear the children crying?
Do you not see their tears?
In their eyes you can read their fears
Of sorrow and suffering too gruesome for their years.

Every day there are children dying
From booze and drugs which they are buying.
Shattered dreams in the graves are lying.
Come on child, Live! Why aren't you even trying?

Hear their groans, feel their pain!
To ignore them is inhumane.
Their extinction would be our loss
So we must protect them at all costs.

Can't you hear their silent call/
Please…someone answer- don't let them fall.
It's our duty, one and all,
To teach them pride; help them stand tall.

Love them: don't abuse them.
Listen: don't accuse them.
Guidance: don't refuse them.
Save them or we will lose them.

Hear the children.

Wednesday, November 27, 1991

(Sunday, 12/29/2013
I actually composed this poem during the Spring semester of 1981 when I was a freshman at the University of Miami. It was my 2nd semester and I volunteered at the Big Brothers Big Sisters program. But it was not until 1991 that I finally put it on paper.)

<u>The Direction of a Child</u>
(Dedicated to 12 year old O.S.)

Bright…
A visionary but more than that –
A dreamer with hopes and aspirations.

Strong family ties:
His source of love, strength and inspiration –
A sense of knowing and of being somebody.

A performer,
But more than that!
An achiever not just a believer.

Young male child…
Gifted…
Black.

Sunday, 4/4/93

(Sunday, 12/29/13 - I met Omar S. while I worked at the Port Authority Bus Terminal in Manhattan. During our first encounter, I stopped him because I was concerned that he would be easy prey for child predators, especially since he was travelling alone. I also

wanted to make sure that he was not a runaway. I made him call his mom and she informed me that she was a nurse and worked during the hours that he had to travel. On Sundays, he would leave home to go to this prep school in upstate NY. On Fridays, he would return to his mom's home for the weekends. We made an agreement, that whenever he was in the Terminal, he would stop at my booth and wait until it was time for him to board the bus. During his wait time, he would do some art work, or math or science. I would then walk him to the gate. Twenty years later, as I write this note, my prayer is that he fulfilled the call of destiny on his life to be a successful young man.)

To a Friend
(Dedicated to my co-worker Denis Knaack)

Something caught my eye at work this morning
That really touched my heart.
Seeing what I saw was really not expected
And it gave me quite a start.

There on the table was a roll of tissue
Wrapped in ribbons of purple, pink and blue.
Attached was a note with a very brief message
And I knew it was put there by you.

The note simply stated: "just a little something
To remember me by when I am gone."
And then when I saw you, I asked how you were feeling
Knowing only a little of the struggle you'd begun.

You tried to hide your feelings but your face told the story
Of fear and uncertainty and life's ambiguity.
As you tore up the note and threw away the pieces
I wished in some way I could set your mind at

ease.

These past months I have watched you and I've listened.
So while there's still time, as a friend, I'd like to mention:
In your every waking hour, make each second count.
Each kind thought, word, and deed: let these be your legacy.

Tuesday, 7/28/92

(Sunday, 12/29/2013 - I wrote this poem for my co-worker Denis at a time when the HIV/AIDS epidemic was at an all time high. He had recently learned that he had AIDS. I heard it through the grapevine at work and it broke my heart to see how he was being treated. He faced several hurdles: alienation by the heterosexual population, judgment by religious folk and just plain meanness on the part of people with their nasty looks and gossip, people who were fearful that they would get what he had just by being near him.

Up to the time of this poem, I had been co-workers with Denis for 8 years. He knew I was a Christian, a quiet woman, African American. He was Caucasian, very outgoing and loved to tell jokes. He kept his jokes clean whenever I was around. So, on that early Tuesday morning, when I saw the roll of tissue, I hesitantly approached him, not wanting to intrude without permission, not knowing how he would respond to my genuine inquiry. I didn't see the differences between us. The question in my mind was, how would Jesus treat him? All I saw was a suffering human being whom God loved and I was willing to lend a helping hand or a listening ear. Denis and I became more than co-workers on that day. We became friends.)

The Passing of a Friend

During the past 10 years that I'd known Bernie, I came to realize that when he was around, there was never a dull moment. There was always something done or said that would bring a smile to your face. When I first met Bernie, I soon became the recipient of his many pranks. At first I would be so upset, wondering why he was picking on me. I quickly learned that he was harmless.

In the scriptures, in the book of Proverbs, there is a verse which states: "A merry heart doeth good like a medicine, but a broken spirit drieth up the bones." I can truly say that Bernie Miles was one of those rare people with a merry heart. From the glimpses that I gleaned from his life, I observed that he was one who not only LOVED life but also lived life (and to the fullest). He will be missed. Therefore I dedicate this poem to his memory.

It was early dawn
On Tuesday morn.
In fact.....
5:49 to be exact.

Just before I signed in, the supervisor said,
"Tracy, have you heard that Bernie Miles is dead?"
(Everything seemed "just right" in the world,
So I wasn't quite prepared for what I had just

heard).

Shocked into silence, my senses were reeling.
Stunned into oblivion, I was left without feeling.

“Bernie Miles dead? When did this happen?”
Last Thursday,” she replied, “it was all of a sudden.”
Bernie Miles, gone? I quietly reflected,
No…it can’t be! This is not what I expected.

It was hard to believe I’d never hear his voice again.
Still harder to conceive I’d never see his smile again.

Full of life, charm and wit
And a style all his own,
He was known for his generous spirit
And for the strength that he passed along.

Bernie Miles…gone, to meet his Maker in the sky,
Someday we hope to see him in the great by and by.

And though, in this round, death may have finally won,
Each kind word, thought and deed: his legacy lives on.

Wednesday 7/20/94

(Sunday, 12/29/13
It has been almost 20 years since Bernie's death. I learned shortly before his death that he was battling the AIDS epidemic. For years, he had lived what is now known as the down low lifestyle, married to a woman with several grown children. Later in his life, he "came out" as a gay man, still very active in his church. The disease hit him hard: he went from a vibrant man to one who quickly lost weight and succumbed to its deadly blows.)

Silent Rage

By Gerard McBean*

Although the rage in my heart
Screams out;
My mouth utters not a word.
Although the pain I feel
Scars not the body,
My mind tells me
To give in –
But my pride tells me
To persevere:
For it won't be long.
Oppression is a dirty word
For….in any race we are
All children of God
And there will come
A day when the
Slate is wiped clean
And these words that tarnish
The lords' wish list
Will vanish as if it
Was never there.

*Gerard McBean, co-worker at the Port Authority of Y and NJ

Untitled

By Gerard McBean*

In this day and age
Of money-mongers and pleasure-seekers,
The colors of the rainbow
Are classified into divisions
And sub-divisions
To show the power of the pocket
While looking straight ahead
And being blind-sided of what has been there for years.

Religion, Color and Characteristics are
Items sold in the store of life.
To reject the truth
And accept the lie,
Eyes are blinded with lust
Of others as generations of Kings
Die….lost….never to rule.

Life's poisonous bite
Strikes, affecting the uneducated,
The needy and the too-poor to realize

(the) 50 days of life.
Disaster starts at day one….
Sons of crack….
Never to have half a chance.

*Gerard McBean, co-worker at the Port Authority of NY and NJ

INDIGNATION!!!

When the burdens of life seem
    To weigh you down,
And all of your smiles are turned
    Into frowns,
When injustice and evil men fill
    You daily with fear,
And the cross that you carry seems
    Harder to bear;

Refuse Resignation –
Don't you dare give up!
Choose indignation –
Fight with all your might and keep looking up.

Saturday, 9/11/93

JUSTICE

Justice

Undeniably

Shall someday succeed

Tremendously to,

Inevitably,

Conquer

Evil.

Tuesday, 12/15/92

Be Faithful, Be Grateful

As I sat pondering over life's affairs
Brows creased with anxiety, worries and cares,
I heard a voice whisper so quiet and low:
"Be careful for nothing; pray and give thanks.
Tell God all your troubles, He owns all the
banks."

This I considered when to my surprise,
I heard the Lord say, "In this you must be wise.
Fretting and doubting change nothing you know.
Be grateful instead for all the little things;
Like life, health and strength and the joy each day
brings."

God sends the sunshine as well as the rain.
He's touched with our infirmities, He feels every
pain!
Though satan should buffet, God softens each
blow.
So give all to Jesus and rest in His peace,
Then climb every mountain with the greatest of
ease.

Be faithful and loyal in all that you do.
You're in the Master's service so to Him you must be true.
Keep your eyes towards heavens, resisting the foe.
Fight the good fight of faith and finish your course,
In the end there's a crown that is eternally yours.

Tuesday, 12/3/91

Excuses but not Excused

So you say you're not worthy to be used by the Lord,
That you need more time, more anointing before you preach His Word.
But I heard in my spirit, "quit making excuses.
While you sit there complaining the devil is gaining
A stronghold in some poor soul's life."

Walk worthy of the vocation wherewith you are called.
Endure hardness as a good soldier, be strong and stand tall.
Put on the whole armor and take the abuses.
More intense than basic training and from blows you may be paining,
In the end you'll have eternal life.

Excuses but not excused not even when Christ you fail,
For on Calvary He shed His blood and in so doing posted our bail.

So preach to the sinner though God's word he refuses:
Himself to death he will be chaining while you yourself will be obtaining
A fast hold on eternal life.

Monday, 1/28/91

Stay in the Race

Jesse Owens, Carl Lewis, Mohammed Ali;
Flo-Jo, Wilma Rudolph, Jackie-Joyner-Kersee:
Each in his or her own way had a race to run –
A race against time at the sound of a bell or gun.

Countless hours and years of training mixed with blood, sweat and tears,
In order to be true winners they had to conquer many fears.
Winning they knew, of course, would be very sweet.
But they also had to be ready for the agony of defeat.

In our own race with time from the cradle to the grave,
Ever-growing, ever-learning, we must try to be brave.
Each of us *must* run, not relying on a friend.
This race is won, not by might or power, but by enduring to the end.

Stay in the race.

Saturday, 12/5/92

Give Him Your All

When you've tried everything to gain happiness,
But somehow it eludes you and you're without
success;

Give Christ your all, He won't let you fall.
For after a while you can stand strong and tall.

Saturday, 12/5/92

Abba: Father

Abba: Father; the One from whom my inspiration extends.
Abba: Father; the One to whom I turn when my world seems at an end.

Abba: Father; my hope, my joy, my peace.
Abba: Father; in whom my faith is released.

Abba: Father; who knows my very thoughts,
Especially at those times when I'm at a loss for words.

Abba: Father; my shelter in the time of storms.
Abba: Father; my solid rock on which I stand.

Abba: Father – Jesus – my trust is in you.

Monday, 6/7/82

Thank God for Life's Hardships

Three days ago, I was in Prospect Park with my children. Suddenly a dog raced past us and jumped into the lake to cool off from the heat. It was not until he emerged from the lake, dripping with water, did I observe that his right hind leg was totally amputated.

But that didn't stop him from enjoying life! He shook himself off and raced back to his owners who readily received him with shouts of love.

How much more should we, as human beings, appreciate life and thank God, daily, in spite of life's hardships.

Thursday, 4/11/91

In the Palm of His Hands

I've cried many tears in the past days,
wondering if I should end it all.
Has my life any real meaning?
Have I been obedient, have I really been called?

Who really cares if I live or die?
My husband? My son? Or the one I'm carry inside?
No one knows the sorrow I feel.
No one knows of the pain that's so real.

The smile I war…it's just a façade –
A mask that hides all of the aches inside.
I silently pray for death to please come.
But each morning I'm disappointed when the sky greets the sun.

I cry: "Lord leave me alone; please, go away.
I don't want to talk for I've nothing to say."

But, Oh1 for a love that will not die!
Oh1 for a love that won't be pushed aside!

Even in my torment You minister to me –
For from deep within You sing to me.
Jesus loves me, this I know, for the Bible tells me so.
Little ones to Him belong: they are weak but He is strong.

I try to drown you out of all my thoughts.
But still louder Your voice rings out even more:
"Sweet Hour of Prayer", "I must tell Jesus;"
"Oh how I love Jesus", and "What a Friend."

Slowly the battle within me subsides.
Gently You dry the tears from my eyes.
Softly You tell me, "*Stand to your feet.*
Tracy, My work, you first must complete."

"Be strong in the Lord and in the power of His might.
Put on the whole armor and prepare to fight.
Now of your own strength you cannot prevail-
But through Christ you can do all and you will never will fail.

"Lo, I'm with you always even to the end.
I'll stick closer to you than any brother or friend."
And though there are times when I may not understand,
One thing is for sure, I'm IN THE PALM OF HIS HAND.

Monday, 3/2/87

Wednesday, January 1, 2014:
As I type these words this New Year's Day, I think back to that time in my life. At that time, I had a three year old son. I was newly married in September 1986 and by March of 1987I was six months pregnant. (Yup, got pregnant on our honeymoon night...lol) I was the victim of domestic violence which lasted until I finally left a few days after Christmas 1990.

During that marriage, I was renting an apartment from my church and there were many times that the pastor would witness the abuse but turn a blind eye and a deaf ear to my cries. I experienced physical violence while pregnant with both my daughters. I went into early labor while six months pregnant with my first daughter but got to the hospital in time so that the labor was stopped. The doctors placed me on bed rest until three months after she was born. With my second daughter, I was beaten so badly and again went in to early labor. I was hemorrhaging by the time I got to the hospital and had a caesarean section. She was born twelve weeks early, weighing only 2 pounds 2 ounces.

Please note that during that period of my life, we spent more months separated than we did living under the same roof. I did my best to keep us together, believing his lies and his "I'm sorry". We went to counseling at my church but I was told that I was not being a proper wife or fulfilling his needs. He was a drug addict and an alcoholic but I was made to feel that I was the culprit. He was no longer working and every penny I worked for, he would steal. He would also break into neighbors' houses and I would have to pay them back for any damage or stolen properties.

Not only did I have to deal with the abuse at the hands of my husband, I was alienated from family members. I felt the hypocrisy of church members who through their silence condoned his behavior or through sermons from the pulpit would spout words such as "wives ought to obey and submit to their husbands". I finally got the courage to leave for good after the Christmas of 1990 when he stole all the gifts, sold the television, my son's dog, fur coat, winter clothing, living room furniture, and anything that could not be nailed down. I fortified myself with the knowledge that God was not the cause of the abuse nor did it please Him that

I continue in the abuse.

Since that time, I have become stronger. I have overcome other obstacles: rape of my youngest daughter by a stranger when she was only twelve years old; her ensuing suicide attempts on at least four occasions; runaway for almost three years; reunited with her but the struggles that came from my woman-child who was now a 'stranger' with destructive habits and behaviors; having to deal with her anger and being the object of her wrath, the ensuing accusations and manipulations. But I assured and reassured her that I had too much invested in her, that she was still my princess. Her status had not changed. I also finally accepted the fact that I was not to blame for the tragedy,

My children are now grown and leading honest, productive lives. Though there have been many scars, the healing continues, one day at a time.)

Songs in the Night

Often in my life, I have gone through some very trying experiences. Times when my heart has been so overwhelmed that I've had to turn to the Rock that is higher than I. Times when I couldn't even put into words the agony of my soul. There were times when I'd been hurt so badly that it felt like everything was closing in on me, as if the world was spinning so fast and I wanted to get off of the rollercoaster ride but was utterly helpless to do so.

Oh those times! Those were times when I could only say "Jesus", "Oh Jesus", and "Oh Jesus". During those times, the night seemed so dark that I would actually pray for day. Then the Lord would cause me to remember that "even the night shall be light about me" (Psalm 139:11). And I'd say, *yes Lord, but how long before the day?*

During those times there were a few friends who would try to comfort me with scriptures like "weeping may endure for the night, but joy cometh in the morning" (Psalm 30:5). And I'd know that what they said was true. But what they didn't understand was that I needed joy right then.

I have learned that there are times when God doesn't wait until the morning to give joy I so desperately needed. I would be feeling down and during the wee hours of the night, I'd be up wrestling…tossing…talking to my Jesus. I'd start off singing, *Precious Lord take my hand, lead me on help me stand. I am tired, I am weak, I am worn. Through the storm, through the night, lead me on to the light. Take my hand, Precious Lord and lead me on.* I knew right then and there what the author of that song was feeling when he wrote it. (Mr. Thomas A. Dorsey had experienced one trial after another, and to top it all off, he had just lost his wife. I could feel the Spirit of God…moving…gently soothing and comforting me. I had done what David had done when he wrote in Psalm 77:6, "I call to remembrance my **song in the night**: I commune with mine heart; and my spirit made diligent search." I had been comforted in recalling God's mighty deeds towards me.

At other times, Jesus Himself would encourage me to hold on…. To make sure that my anchor was holding and gripping the solid Rock. Slowly the anxiety and the fear would subside and I knew that He had kept his promise and I need not fear the night's terror (Psalm 91:15).

I have come to appreciate those **songs in the night**. These are the times when the Lord encourages me to persevere. My dependence has been solely on Him and He deserves all the praise. I have learned to not panic, thus finding myself swimming against an unrelenting current, an unbeatable foe. I have learned in my hours of distress, sorrow and woe that God is in fact working on my behalf, perfecting that which concerns me.

As I thirst for Him, the Lord is commending His

lovingkindness in the daytime, and “**in the night His song** shall be with me, and my prayer unto the God of my life” ((Psalm 42:8). I have found that God is indeed faithful to His Word when He says in Isaiah 30:29 that “ye shall have **a song as in the night** when a holy solemnity is kept; and gladness of heart, as when one goeth with a pipe to come into the mountain of the Lord, to the Mighty One of Israel.” Unlike Elihu in Job 35:10, there is no need for me to question because I KNOW where Jesus, my Maker, is and I KNOW that He gives **SONGS IN THE NIGHT**.

Friday, 2/22/91

Renewed Strength

I believed in you.
I thought you were my friend.
We laughed, cried and ate together.
I was sure on you I could depend.

I loved you.
For you I'd do anything, gladly giving up my life.
Climb every mountain, cross every valley.
We made a great team: I was glad to be your wife.

We dreamed dreams and painted pictures,
Even building castles in the sky.
Together we would conquer the world –
Together we'd get our share of "a piece of the pie."

But…. All of that is gone now.
Like a vapor of smoke it's vanished away!
Like the morning dew in the early dawn,
Like the very first snowflakes on a cold winter's day.

Broken promises and shattered dreams;
Words and actions all full of deceit.
Drugs and booze destroyed the home we had
built.
Life seemed harder; I was totally beat.

Out of despair, hope came alive!
With faith in Christ, I would continue to strive.
In the midst of the turmoil, tranquility arrived –
I accepted the unchangeable; I knew I would
survive.

Having learned patience, my strength has been
renewed.
Mounting up as an eagle, I'm beginning to soar!
Facing each challenge with a new-found courage
I have the propensity (and with an intensity) to
live life like never before!

With a new lease on life and a new determination
I can weather the storms for I've learned self-
preservation.

With God as my guide and my children as my inspiration
I've the strength to be me without reservation.

Sunday, 11/19/1989

Road to Recovery

Lord,

On my road to recovery

Of spiritual and emotional healing,

Help me to not become so focused on myself

That I forget those who have stood by me.

Let me not become inconsiderate and selfish or

Neglectful of those who truly love me.

Sunday, 1/31/93

(Thursday, January 02, 2014:
I wrote this short poem shortly after I terminated a relationship of almost two years with a man who was recovering from addiction to drugs and alcohol. While I applauded his days of sobriety which, at this writing, have become more than 20 years of being clean, the

difficulty in our relationship back then was his self-engrossment, self-absorption. It was as if he had forgotten his support system, those who cheered him on daily. He felt that he had made it without the help of those who prayed for him, who welcomed him back when he had lapses, who cleaned him up when he came home filthy drunk and high off of drugs, crack cocaine. His sole focus was NA and AA and those who were fellow addicts and alcoholics, very often the ones who were with him when he had a relapse. He would tell me stories of being at an AA or NA meeting and often going into the bathroom to "hook up" with another attendee.

While we were together, he went back to college. It was during a break in semesters, when he had nothing to keep his focus, he lapsed and became abusive. I had to end the relationship then because my safety and that of my three children were of utmost importance. He later attained his Associate degree and since attained his Bachelor and Master's degrees. I was (am) so proud of him.

But I had my own road to recovery, howbeit, from low self-esteem and from that of domestic violence. Though I have never used/abused drugs or alcohol, I still had to recover emotionally and spiritually.

So my prayer when I wrote this was to be thankful and never forget those precious loved ones who are always encouraging me to be the best that I am, that I need them to survive.)

The Road to Success
By Gerard McBean*

The Road to Success
Is full of twists and turns
And forks in the road, (some)
Leading to endless loops
While the others lead you to
The treasures you search for.
So when you encounter this
Fork, stand strong and
Follow the Lord.

*Gerard McBean, co-worker at the Port Authority of NY and NJ

Having Done All To Stand, Stand

Having done all to stand, stand.

Stand through the trials and tribulations, knowing that the trial of your faith, which is more precious than gold that perishes, will be unto praise and honor at the Lord's appearing.

Stand for He told us that He has already overcome the world.

Stand even when men revile and persecute you, even when they curse, hate and use you. Stand, and be not weary in well doing for you shall reap in due season if you faint not. Remember, great is your reward in heaven.

And in standing, run that you may obtain, pressing toward the mark for the prize of the high calling of God in Christ Jesus.

And in running, do it with patience, laying aside every weight, looking unto our beloved Saviour who is the author and finisher of our faith. Keep in mind that the race is given to him who endures to the end.

Having on the whole armor of God, let us continue to fight the good fight of faith, for in the end we shall receive a crown of righteousness.

As we fight, we learn that the battle is really the Lord's, so we can stand still and see His salvation with us. We can stand still and know that He is God.

Stand even when we are chastened of the Lord. It may not be joyous for the moment, but it is for our profit that we may be partakers of His Holiness yielding the peaceable fruit of righteousness.

Stand regardless of how hot the fire because He will take the heat out of the flame. We need not fear for He has redeemed us and called us by His name. Although we may pass through the waters and the rivers, they shall not overflow us. When we walk through the fire, we will not be burned.

Having done all to stand, STAND.

Wednesday, 8/15/84

Remember Now Thy Creator

"Remember now thy Creator in the days of thy youth."

So wrote the preacher in the 12th chapter of Ecclesiastes. It was necessary that he wrote this because, too often, being young, we forget just how good God has been to us. Many times we neglect to lay aside worry and every weight and sin which doth so easily beset us.

Remember....This means that we are to call to mind the lovingkindness of the Lord. We are to keep in mind that His mercy endures forever. We are to take care not to forget that His faithfulness is renewed toward us every morning. We are to think again by an act of our memory that great is the Lord and greatly to be praised. He is worthy to be remembered.... "REMEMBER now thy Creator in the days of thy youth."

Now....This means at the present moment. Testify now of how He woke us up this morning. Tell it on the mountains, the hilltops, and in the valleys of how Jesus came all the way down from glory to save one such as you and I. Tell it… now… on the highways and byways, even if they won't listen or even if they don't believe you. Tell them… now, how He loves them and He came to let them know….Tell them also of His judgment on those who reject Him…. "Remember NOW thy Creator in the days of thy youth."

Creator….our Lord and our God. The One who causes us to be, giving us a new name and a new heart of flesh. The One in whom we are no longer condemned. The One in whose image we were created and now are new creatures. Old things are passed away – all is become new. Our Creator, by whom our minds are being transformed by the washing of the water by the Word…. "Remember now thy CREATOR in the days of thy youth."

Youth….Remember Him now while we are young and in the early part of life where our senses are at their peak: our eyes are not yet dimmed; our ears are not yet dulled. Remember Him especially in our spiritual growth, growing from carnally-minded babes to mature Christians, having searched the scriptures and rightly dividing the Word of Truth. We are to remember Him in our youth and to do with all our might and strength whatever our hands find to do. However, not glorying in our own strength or might, rather glorying in Christ and that we understand and know HIM, the only True God. Let our boast always be in Him…. "Remember now thy Creator in the days of thy YOUTH."

Wednesday, July 18, 1984

You're My Inspiration

You inspire me, Lord.
Your love takes me higher
Until my desire
Is to acquire
Your attributes.

Of your Word I
never grow tired.
For it is like a fire –
A purifier – that purges me
So that I become all that
You require.

Thursday, 8/13/92

Daddy's Eyes

Every time I see daddy
There's something special in his eyes.
Like a twinkle or a sparkle
From the stars up in the skies.

His eyes, they tell the story
Of past battles lost and won.
And if I take the time to listen
I learn how to cope with this life I've begun.

He's not a man who talks much,
In fact his words are very few.
But when he speaks it is with wisdom
Designed to help and not hinder you.

Yes, every time I see daddy
There's something special in his eyes:
Like love and understanding
And the simple joy of life.

Monday, 12/14/92
(Friday, January 03, 2014:
My father passed away June 24, 2010. He is missed dearly but lives forever in our hearts.)

Take Care of Mama

For the countless times you encouraged me,
And the sleepless nights you watched over me;
For the many tears that you shed for me,
And the many prayers that you prayed for me:

I want you to know that I can never repay
For all of the sacrifices that you have made.
You've taught me, most of all, how to live and be strong –
And one day I'll take care of you like deserve.

Sunday, 12/13/92

(Friday, January 03, 2014:
I thank God for my mom. I love her dearly and am so proud of how she raised 5 young girls in the projects, in the heart of Brooklyn, NY. Things weren't always easy, and there were times when I experienced abuse at her hands, I have forgiven her and forgiven me.

Even as a parent myself, I have made mistakes, but thankful to God that I did not abuse or break their spirits. When I was wrong or jumped to conclusions and grounded them for some infraction before hearing all of the facts, I have asked their forgiveness. I believe in transparency and encouraged dialogue from the time they were babies. Whether angry or happy, I strived to make home a place of safety and love, where no conversation was taboo. Each evening, we would sit down to eat and each person told how their day was, good or bad.

Again, I thank God for my mom and will always love her.)

Brothers

Brave:
Ready always to defend their sibling's honor; but
Often a source of merriment and fun.
Trustworthy –
Helpful when needed but never
Engulfing or overwhelming;
Respecting one's decisions. A
Source of stability and strength.

Saturday, 2/20/93

(Friday, January 03, 2014:
I have 2 blood brothers, Jeremy and Marcus. Both are great and I love them immensely. However, over the years, there have been other "brothers" I could always call when I needed to vent or understand the male psyche a little better. Thank God for Gary, Gerard, George, and Kevin. You're simply the best.)

SISTERS

Sisters are
Inseparable in
Spite of their differences;
They are there always to
Encourage and
Reassure you to follow your dreams.
SOAR like the eagle! Reach your highest height.

Saturday, 2/20/93

(Friday, January 03, 2014:
I have 5 blood sisters whom I love dearly: my twin sister Terri, Bridget, Mildred, Rochelle (also my best friend), and Tina. But there are several women that God placed in my life that are very dear to me: Levita, Allison, Canena (who passed away last March), Monique and Litta. Thanks for being unconditional in your love and acceptance of me, and giving not only encouragement and strength when needed, but also allaying any fears and straightening me out when necessary.)

My Firstborn

He has the sweetest of smiles
    That brightens any room.
And a heart full of love
    That causes flowers to bloom.

He's loving and caring
    To both the rich and the poor.
And if he were able
    No one would suffer anymore.

Poverty, hate and homelessness
    To him - they are a crime,
And one day he intends to solve them
    It's only a matter of time.

Jonathan is his name -
    This means "gracious gift of God."
To this child we're all the same:
    No one is better, no one is odd.

He can be stubborn and strong-willed
    With a mind of his own.

Though he's nine, yet he's determined
        To make a difference when he's grown.

With joy in the face of sorrow
        And hope for tomorrow,
Despite life's uncertainties
        He'll have strength to meet each foe.

Friday, 2/19/93

(Friday, January 03, 2014:
I am simply amazed that after 21 years of writing this poem, how true the words are. Dare I say prophetic? My son is now a Licensed Massage Therapist, about to open his own practice. He previously served in the US Navy for five years. He has two wonderful daughters. But again, God is simply wonderful in the way, the path that He has lead Jonathan. I can't wait to see how the next 21 years unfold.)

My Little Bee, Miss Dee

Her name is Deborah which means "busy as a bee",
And like her little namesake, she is just as industrious.
Quick to learn, full of charm and just a curious –
She's my little bee, Miss Dee.

Being loving and giving, she's truly a "Friday's child,"
But please don't get her angry or she'll sit and pout for a while.
She can be as sweet as honey with the sweetest of smiles –
She's my little bee, Miss Dee.

Miss Dee is strong-willed (or stubborn) with a very strong spirit.
She doesn't give up easily, she just doesn't quit.
Although she's only five, she has both style and wit –
Yes….she's my little bee, Miss Dee!

Saturday, 12/5/92

(Friday, January 03, 2014:

Wow, talk about living out the meaning of her name, Deborah has done just that. During the Christmas holidays, she buys gifts for all the children that she knows even though she has none of her own.She even buys gifts for the grownups. The reality is that she is always giving of herself, even when she has worked several jobs and may me tired, she will get up to help a friend in need. She is fiercely protective of family and friends. When provoked, she is capable of setting the record straight, but always done in love and in a no-nonsense manner. You never have to worry where she stands on any issue. She speaks her mind from a place of honesty and truth, able to see many sides of an argument. Quite the lady, my Diva Princess!)

Elizabeth's Victory

Elizabeth = consecrated to or promised of God.

She was born twelve weeks early before her time,
So she learned very early how to survive.
Even when it seemed all hope was gone,
She didn't give up, she continued to strive.

Dependent on God for every breath that she breathed,
I took nothing for granted: Ask and you shall receive."
I watched her grow stronger and stronger each day.
The courage she showed gave me strength to believe.

Over seven long weeks she grew from two pounds to five –
The day to take her home had finally arrived!
There was joy and happiness in our home that spring morn
Because my precious little girl had finally come

home.

It has been four years and I must admit,
sometimes things were rough.
She's had two operations which have served to
make her tough.
She's gentle and kind, full of life and very sweet –
I thank God for her and for making my life
complete.

Wednesday, 12/16/92

(Friday, January 03, 2014:
All I can say is that God is truly amazing over how He has kept Elizabeth these many years. From the time she was born, she has been a fighter, victorious. Even after the rape, the ensuing suicide attempts, the runaway period shortly thereafter from ages 13 to 16, the return home, earning her GED with a 3.4 GPA, overcoming huge hurdles, she is still a survivor. Like Joseph, I can say, that what the adversary meant for evil against my daughter, God has worked out for good and for His glory. I stand back in awe as I watch the Lord Jesus Christ complete His great work in her, in all of my children.)

Talent Spectacular
(Boys Choir of Harlem)

Welcome, welcome
To our Talent Spectacular,
Where song reigns supreme
And rap is our vernacular.
Here, comedy is king –
As you soon will see.
We have a great show planned:
I hope you will agree.
So clap your hands
And feel the beat!
Listen to the music
Of our dancing feet.

Welcome!

Tuesday, 6/22/93

(Friday, January 03, 2014:
My son attended the Boys Choir of Harlem Academy and sang in their choir for 4 years. This was one of the speeches I wrote for him for one of their end-of-year programs. It would be great one day to see them and how they have progressed.)

Happiness

By Gerard McBean*

Happiness has no boundaries –
For boundaries are only
Man-made obstacles
Set up to bewilder the mind.

Set aside these boundaries
And lunge forward –
For happiness never knocks.

Pursue your goal,
Never letting the lesser-
Minded hold you back.

*Gerard McBean, co-worker at the Port Authority of NY and NJ

Friendship
By Gerard McBean*

Friendship is far beyond
A casual hand-shake
Or a cheerful hello.

Friendship is tow
People enjoying each other's company for the
Sake of fun, laughter
And wholesome strength.
So, as a friend, enjoy it all
Because this is priceless gold.

*Gerard McBean, co-worker at the Port Authority of NY and NJ

Together, Forever & Always

Winter, spring, summer or fall:
The seasons may change but never will my love.
January, February, March through December:
The months may change but never will my love.

My love for you is a fire: a flame on a candle.

With each passing day that flame grows and grows
Without shame for all the world to see.
The rains will come, the storms will rise:
But they cannot quench that flame of love.

My love can never be diminished.
As a flame, it can never be extinguished.
For with each new day, I go to the Source – Jesus –
And he renews my love with His love.

I will love…always…love you.
As we grow older, our kind of love will never grow old.

Our minds and spirits will be molded as one & so will our bodies –
One mind, one spirit, one flesh.

You and me.

Together, Forever & Always…

Sunday, 11/1/81

(Friday, January 03, 2014:
As I read this poem, I can't help but laugh out loud at my naiveté! Whew. When I wrote this in 1981, I was engaged to my son's father. I was attending the University of Miami and that fall semester I was a sophomore. Quite frankly, I had not even experienced sexual love, I was a virgin, still "wet" behind the ears, and seven days shy of my 20th birthday. A year after writing this, I got pregnant. We never did marry.

I applaud my innocence at that age; I also applaud the journey I have taken.to get to where I am now. Though I have not found Mr. Right yet, I am grateful for the relationships and yes marriages I have had, however few!! I applaud the fact that I still believe in romantic love, but it is unconditional love that lasts through decades, and endures the hardships.

Note to self: keep on believing, something wonderful is about to happen…just around the bend!!)

For You My Love

Your gentle smile;
Your tender kiss;
Your warm embrace:
I can't resist.

When I'm in your arms
You're full of charm.
Your love takes me higher –
You really inspire.

You give me strength:
You're so full of life.
There's never a dull moment;
No confusion or strife.

You're thoughtful and earnest
Loyal and true.
For the man that you are
Sweetheart, I love you.

Friday, 2/19/93

Passion

Powerful
And Arduous emotions;
Sensuously, Sensually Stimulating – Sometimes
Spiritually Satisfying.
Intoxicatingly Inviting but
Often for just a moment. Of
Necessity Needing constant rejuvenation or it
simply…fades…away…

Friday, 10/14/94

(Friday, January 03, 2014:
I wrote this poem when a male friend of mine kept talking about passion and I wanted him to know that in any relationship, passion is good but it is not the glue to keeping the relationship together. If there is to be longevity, there are other elements that are needed, i.e.: communication, acceptance, unconditional love, etc.)

Touching the World through Love

In these days and times, one cannot help but see that we are living in the last days. These are perilous times: men love themselves, loving pleasures more than they love God or their fellowman. We see that because iniquity is in such abundance, the love of many has grown cold. In fact, many people are too afraid to love. How then can we even begin to love, let alone touch the world through love?

Let us take a look at two individuals who were able to do just that. They overcame their enemies and effectively touched the world through love.

Mahatma Gandhi, leader of the oppressed peoples of India under British rule. He believed in non-violence as a means of effecting change in the government. His love for his people (and his enemies) was embedded deep within him. Had this not been the case, he could not have uttered in his words to his assassin, "I forgive you my son."

Next we see Dr. Martin Luther King, Jr. He was the leader of the Civil Rights Movement during the 1950s and 1960s in the United States. In the words of the Constitution, he believed that all men (black and white) were "created equal, that they are endowed by their Creator with certain inalienable rights. That among these are life, liberty, and the pursuit of happiness." And that "whenever any form of government becomes destructive to these ends, it is the right of the people to alter or abolish it, and to institute a new government, laying its foundation on such principles."

In his book, Strength to Love, Dr. King wrote that the best way to win your enemy was to befriend him. He further stated that rather than hating our oppressors and risk becoming like them, African Americans were to love them, thus rising above them.

Now let us look at Jesus, the epitome of love. He loved us so much that while we were yet sinners, He died for us. Rather than condemn a woman to die, He told her to go and sin no more. All that He commanded us to do, there was not anything that He Himself did not do.

His lovingkindness drew us. By His example, He taught His disciples how to love. The change that Christ effected in their lives was so evident that it was later said of them that they were turning the world upside down (for Christ).

Jesus' greatest expression of love was exhibited on Calvary's cross. In His dying hour, He uttered words that echo down through the centuries: *Father, forgive them for they know not what they do."* These words still give mankind hope.

How then can **we** touch the world through love? By lifting up the name of Jesus so that He can do the drawing of souls. By allowing self to decrease and Christ to increase the more in our lives. By loving one another because this is what identifies us as Christians. By being available to meet the needs of a dying world….first naturally. In so doing, we open the door to preparing their hearts to receive the word of God, thus meeting their spiritual needs.

We need not be ashamed of the gospel of Jesus Christ especially in times of persecution and mockery by the world. For we know that the gospel is the power of God unto salvation to everyone that believes.

Let us touch the world through love.

Wednesday, June 27, 1990

www.ingramcontent.com/pod-product-compliance
Lightning Source LLC
Chambersburg PA
CBHW062025040426
42447CB00010B/2145